Hillstrom's Merchandise Forensics

A Case Study In Understanding Why Merchandising Issues Impact
Marketing Productivity And Business Health

Kevin Hillstrom

Acknowledgements

I would like to thank my loyal clients, who helped make Merchandise Forensics possible through dozens of interesting and fascinating projects over the past eighteen months.

13 Digit ISBN: 978-1492367499+

Published in the United States of America by Kevin Hillstrom

Available from Amazon.com and other retailers.

Manufactured in the United States of America
First Edition

Cover Design: Kevin Hillstrom and Createspace.com
Cover Art: Kevin Hillstrom

Marketing

I know, I know. You thought you were going to read a booklet on Merchandise Forensics. That's what you purchased, that's what you thought you were going to get. And then Kevin starts the discussion with the word "Marketing".

But that's where our discussion needs to start.

Let's consider a paid search program. You invest $1,000, and you obtain the following results:
- Investment = $1,000.
- Clicks = 2,000.
- Conversion Rate = 2%.
- Average Order Value = $100.
- Profit Factor = 30%.
- Demand = 2,000 * 0.02 * $100 = $4,000.
- Profit = $4,000 * 0.30 - $1,000 = $200.
- Ad-To-Sales Ratio = $1,000 / $4,000 = 25%.

That's not too bad, is it? You made a profit. That's a good thing!

Next year, Management is frustrated. With you! The performance of your paid search program stinks. Look at these metrics:
- Investment = $1,000.
- Clicks = 2,000.
- Conversion Rate = 1.6%.
- Average Order Value = $96.
- Profit Factor = 30%.
- Demand = 2,000 * 0.016 * $96 = $3,072.
- Profit = $3,072 * 0.30 - $1,000 = ($78).
- Ad-To-Sales Ratio = $1,000 / $3,072 = 33%.

Your paid search program is losing money. This is *your* fault!

Of course, there are two metrics that changed, right?

The conversion rate declined, from 2.0% to 1.6%.

And average order value declined, from $100 to $96.

In many companies, the online marketing team is next up in the line of fire. It can't be the fault of the paid search analyst or paid search vendor. Conversion rate declined, so something happened on the website. Average order value declined, too, so it has to be the online marketing folks who messed this one up!

Now, if you head out to Twitter, you'll learn a hundred thousand reasons why your website experience stinks. Everybody is an expert, and they know that the large orange button works better than the small purple button. Somebody runs a test and learns that large images convert better - then somebody else runs a test and learns that small images convert better. Over time, certain themes win seventy percent of the time, becoming best practices.

Except that there's one little problem.

All of this online marketing wizardry and conversion theory doesn't move the needle, on an annual basis.

Seriously.

Heck, I just read a quote where a large business (tens of millions of dollars) just increased conversion rate by more than two hundred percent. And yet, at the end of the year, that business will grow by five percent, or ten percent, or fifteen percent.

The problem with all of this expert commentary about website design is that it ignores the most important reason why a website converts.

A website converts because customers want to buy the merchandise presented to them.

I'm going to say this again.

A website converts because customers want to buy the merchandise presented to them.

We focus on the presentation side of the story, and that's important, no doubt.

We don't focus on the merchandise. Merchandise is more important! Merchandise is most important!

In the example I provided earlier, conversion rates were down, and average order value is down. The combination of conversion rate decline and average order decline resulted in a paid search program that transitioned from profitability to unprofitability.

Is it possible that the merchandise assortment caused this problem? Is it possible that marketing productivity is directly influenced by merchandise productivity? Is it possible that the issue has nothing to do with paid search?

Of course it is!

I don't want to go "old school" on you, but sometimes, I have to. When I worked at Lands' End, way back in the early 1990s (i.e. before Clinton was President), we evaluated every catalog, on a monthly basis. The focus of our evaluation was on the interaction between merchandise and creative. We learned that if we didn't offer the best merchandise at the start of the catalog, the catalog didn't perform well.

Do you think it is possible that if you do not offer the best merchandise on your home page or landing pages, that you will experience a productivity decline? In other words, if you don't offer the best merchandise on a landing page, is it possible that paid search productivity will decline?

Of course it is!

But it goes much deeper than that.

It's not hard to identify the best merchandise *today*. Work with your merchants, find the most productive items, and present them to the customer. Easy.

It is *very hard* to develop a merchandising strategy that will cause the marketer to be able to pick from a high quality merchandise asortment *three years from now*.

In the course of more than twenty-five years of analyzing customer behavior, I've identified just two strategies that cause businesses to thrive.

1. A robust and reasonably inexpensive new customer acquisition program.
2. The ability of a business to consistently introduce, cultivate, and promote new items to best-seller status.

Long-term profit is dependent on each tactic.

Short-term profit, which almost everybody optimizes to a fault, focuses on exploiting existing customers with existing best sellers to increase profitability.

Your current marketing productivity, therefore, is highly dependent upon the decisions made by the Merchandising team several years ago. If your efforts are failing, it's your fault, no doubt. But it is also the fault of your Merchandising team, based on the decisions they made twelve to thirty-six months ago.

Once we realize that marketing productivity is tethered to merchandising tactics, well, we're almost required to view the world differently. For once, the Marketer is not to blame. We hold the Merchant accountable for Marketing performance. And when the Merchant does an amazing job, we hold the Marketer accountable for not pushing down, hard, on the gas pedal.

The Secret

During the past eighteen months, the focus of my projects changed, subtly at first, then more profoundly.

When I started consulting, back in 2007, the focus was entirely on how customers interacted with channels. I worked hard to explain how catalogs interacted with websites, or how websites drove customers into stores. We didn't have a lot of knowledge in this area, so the work focused on providing knowledge.

By the time 2010 rolled around, businesses were struggling to dig out of the rubble of The Great Recession. Profit was important, and my sweet spot was helping businesses achieve profit goals. As a result, my business thrived.

Then 2012 arrived, and mobile finally penetrated the marketplace. When this happened, we were promised (as we always are) that new channels would yield dramatic sales increases. And unless your customer was under the age of 35, as always, the dramatic sales increases failed to materialize. This caused CEOs to start asking me different questions.

- *"Why isn't my business growing? I did everything I was told I should do, and yet, my business is not growing. Please explain to me what is happening."*

This is a humble question, one filled with deeper meaning. The CEO wants to know "the secret" to success - realizing that a series of conversations on social media that drive a customer to a mobile optimized experience fueled by big data is not the answer.

Since the start of 2012, at least twenty (20) projects have centered around the question the CEO asked just a few paragraphs earlier. More than twenty! This is not a coincidence, this is a fundamental shift in how business leaders view marketing performance.

In more than 80% of these projects, I was able to identify a key merchandising issue that held back the business from being successful. Most of the time, the key issue is a lack of focus on developing new merchandise.

Businesses that develop new merchandise today will experience marketing success tomorrow. That's the secret, that's basically what I've learned since the start of 2012. It's a simple concept, really, nothing new. But too few people focus on this aspect of business success.

Because we're all familiar with Apple, we can use Apple as an example of the importance of new merchandise.

- 2001 = iPod.
- 2007 = iPhone.
- 2010 = iPad.

At the time of writing (September 2013), folks are a bit anxious about Apple. There hasn't been a new, breakthrough product in three years, and there isn't a new, breakthrough product on the horizon. Profit is spectacular, as Apple harvests existing products with existing buyers to maximize profit. But new products? That's different, and the experts in the investment community understand this, pounding Apple stock correspondingly.

This trend can be reversed, of course. But what will reverse the trend? New merchandise, of course!

Basically, the past two years have taught me "the secret".
1. New customers are really important. Focus on them while everybody else focuses on existing customers.
2. New merchandise is really important. Those who develop new merchandise today will reap marketing success two or three years from now.
3. Those who measure merchandise productivity learn more about the health of their business than those who measure marketing campaigns.

In this booklet, I am going to focus on methods for understanding merchandise productivity. I am going to demonstrate how I determine if a business has a healthy merchandise assortment. For the nominal fee you paid, you, too, will learn how to determine the impact merchandising issues have on the productivity of your marketing efforts.

Most important, however, is that I want to teach you to think about your business the way a General Manager of a sports team views his/her business. Especially baseball. In baseball, you have a 25 man roster. Then you have a AAA-level team, where your best prospects gain experience. Below that, you have AA teams, high level A teams, low level A teams, and Rookie League teams. If you think of the players on these teams as "merchandise", well, you quickly make the connection. Baseball teams are constantly developing new talent, talent that in two or three years will replace current talent at the Major League level. When teams fail to have a good "farm system", they are forced to overpay for free agent talent, or they just aren't very good, or both!

In football, my favorite team is the Green Bay Packers. Their current General Manager, Ted Thompson, employs a "draft and develop" philosophy, always cultivating young talent that can step in and eventually replace an aging veteran. When a star wide receiver leaves via free agency, earning eight or nine or ten million dollars a year, the "draft and develop" philosophy enables Green Bay to bring in a younger player, at a lower salary, performing at a comparable level.

This "draft and develop" methodology directly relates to merchandise productivity. We must actively evaluate new merchandise today, identifying future "winners", promoting those items, giving them every possible chance to succeed. If we do that well today, then business will perform well two or three years from now. That's the secret. And based on my research over the past two years, almost nobody pays attention to the "draft and develop" methodology that I call "Merchandise Forensics".

The Comp Segment Analysis

Here's the problem with almost all marketing analytics, folks ... they focus on a timeframe that is just too small to matter.

Think about a baseball game, or any sporting event. In baseball, each team gets twenty-seven outs. A baseball season is so random that it takes 162 games of 27 outs each (4,374 outs, total) to get a representative sample that clearly tells how each player, and each team, performed over time. And yet, when you watch your favorite highlight program, sports experts over-analyze individual at bats. This leads to poor conclusions - we can conclude that a .200 hitter does well against a Cy Young Award winning pitcher, because the .200 hitter got one hit in one at-bat ... an essentially random outcome.

In marketing, we have the same problem. We over-analyze marketing campaigns as if they are life and death! Think about it - almost every report we look at measures the performance of a catalog marketing effort, an email marketing campaign, a paid search keyword, or an omnichannel marketing strategy. We measure pieces. When we measure pieces, we miss out on the big picture.

The big picture can be measured, annually. Over the course of the year, the impact of successful campaigns and unsuccessful ones, hundreds of email campaigns and thousands of paid search keywords and millions of tweets is washed out. You're simply left with truth.

A comp segment analysis, based on annual performance, allows us to clearly see how a comparable group of customers performs, averaging out all of the noise of individual marketing campaigns. We're left with truth, the story of why a customer performed better or worse on an annual basis, compared to prior years.

You're free to define your own "comp segment" however you like, there is no right or wrong way to do this. For the majority of my clients (e-commerce, retail, and catalog), the definition is "_exactly two purchases in the prior twelve months_".

Now, here's what I do different than most experts. I freeze the file as of exactly twelve months ago. Then, I identify all the customers purchasing exactly two times in the year prior to that. Finally, I measure how these customers _performed in the next twelve months_. This is the secret sauce that enables the methodology to reveal so many interesting things about customer behavior. The customers are technically equal, so subsequent behavior can only be impacted by three things.

1. Dramatics changes in marketing strategy (which is unlikely for most 2x buyers - they're going to be pummeled with a steady stream of marketing).
2. Changes in the economy (only a huge factor in recessionary times).
3. Changes in merchandise productivity (always an issue).

In other words, the vast majority of differences we find in a comp segment analysis, year-over-year, are going to be caused by differences in merchandise productivity.

Ok, I get it. If you're a statistical guru or big data practitioner, you're probably thinking that this style of defining/segmenting customers is terribly simplistic. Fine. Come up with your own methodology! But for crying out loud, do something! Too few people even bother to measure merchandise productivity. If you come up with an improved way to equalize customer behavior, you'll be able to make your boss/client a fortune, so just do something and stop arguing about the methodology!

With that off my chest, let's continue.

What I am about to present is actual data. This is an actual case study of a business. We're going to learn, via real data, why this business is failing.

Here we go!

I analyzed behavior over the past three years. Let's see what the data reveals.

Year	Freq	Cases	Rebuy	Spend	Value
2013	2	39,923	35.0%	$125.97	$44.12
2012	2	42,416	38.7%	$126.13	$48.75
2011	2	45,438	38.0%	$120.03	$45.56

Already, a story reveals itself. The number of two-time buyers in the past twelve months is on the decline, down from 45,438 two years ago to 39,923 this year. This business is clearly struggling to maintain a loyal customer base.

Next, look at the annual repurchase rate. In the past year, it declined within this audience, from 38.7% to 35.0%. That's a huge drop. This customer audience did not like what it saw! Annual spend per repurchaser is about the same in 2013 as in 2012, though both metrics improved from 2011 (this analysis is for the year ending September 1, 2013 ... 2013 represents 9/1/2012 to 8/31/2013 ... prior years are similarly defined).

When we multiply rebuy rates by spend amounts, we get the annual demand value per buyer. Since rebuy rates dropped significantly in 2013, we see that the value metric is down significantly as well. In 2011, each customer generated $45.56. In 2012, comparable customers generated $48.75. In 2013, comparable customers floated back down to $44.12 per customer.

In many of my projects, I have the luxury of analyzing up to thirteen years of purchase history. When that happens, I get to see an awful lot of interesting trends! In this case, we only have four years of data at our disposal, which allows us to compare three years of comp segment performance. In this case, comp segment performance declined by 9% in 2013, following a 7% increase in 2012. In other words, something positive happened in 2012, something that we will want to explore in more depth. It's important to have perspective when doing Merchandise Forensics work. Often, we fret about performance declines - but those performance declines are simply regressing back to the historical mean. We need to be able to explain that there is a historical trend that we sometimes improve upon, and sometimes fail to achieve.

Let's look at a series of additional metrics.

Year	Freq	Cases	Value	Items per Order	Price per Item	Order per Buyer	Average Order
2013	2	39,923	$44.12	3.95	$20.90	1.53	$82.59
2012	2	42,416	$48.75	3.64	$21.84	1.59	$79.52
2011	2	45,438	$45.56	3.61	$21.07	1.58	$75.95

Recall that comp segment value declined by 9% in 2013. As we look across this series of metrics, we see that Management squeezed an additional 0.31 items per order out of each customer. This corresponds with an approximate $0.96 drop in the price per item purchased. Average order values increased nicely, from $76 in 2011 to $80 in 2012 to $83 in 2013 - but customers chose to order slightly fewer times per year as a consequence.

Average order value is a terribly important sign of the health of a business, in combination with other metrics. When all metrics are suffering, but average order value is growing, we surmise that Management is actively trying to squeeze as much out of the business as is humanly possible, to keep the business afloat.

That certainly appears to be what is happening in this case. Rebuy rates in 2013 are down significantly, and orders per buyer are down marginally. However, average order value increased by about three dollars, keeping comp segment performance at just -9%.

Well, so far we proved that, compared to 2012, business stinks. We have yet to explain *why* it stinks! Let's take a look at this table:

Year	Freq	Cases	Value	Via Promo	No Promo	New Items	Existing Items
2013	2	39,923	$44.12	$25.04	$19.08	$8.98	$35.14
2012	2	42,416	$48.75	$27.79	$20.96	$11.75	$37.00
2011	2	45,438	$45.56	$23.49	$22.07	$12.48	$33.08

There are subtle differences worth paying attention to. Look at the "Via Promo" and "No Promo" columns. In 2011, the mix of demand was nearly equal between demand generated by promotions, and demand generated without the aid of a promotion. But in 2012 and 2013, the mix skews much more toward demand generated via promotions. This is such an important way of looking at a business, folks, and almost nobody does it. Sometimes, we look at the margin impact of a promotion - we denote that gross margin dropped from 62% to 58% ... the difference seems minor and almost unimportant. If we look at demand tied to a promotion, we get a different perspective. In our comp segment view, 52% of 2011 demand was generated via a promotion, while 57% of 2012 and 57% of 2013 demand was generated via a promotion.

In other words, Management tried to prop this business up by offering more and more discounts and promotions. In 2013, the strategy clearly didn't work. But this does explain, in part, why 2012 was better than 2011. Now, in 2013, we're stuck with comparable customer productivity to 2011, but we're also stuck giving away more and more gross margin to keep the business moving forward. Not good. Not good at all.

Again, almost nobody looks at the business in this manner. Why not?

We must look at the business this way. Discounts and promotions are killing e-commerce businesses, one dollar at a time. We just cannot observe this phenomenon when we look at simplistic metrics like conversion rate, gross margin, and ad-to-sales ratio.

Scoot over a couple of columns to the right. Here, we get to see how comp customers performed on newly introduced items, and on existing items. And here, my friends, we get the first inkling of a looming catastrophe.

Look at comp segment performance for existing items.
- 2013 = $35.14.
- 2012 = $37.00.
- 2011 = $33.08.

Compared to two years ago, comp segment performance on existing items is actually +6%. That's not bad. Because the business is experiencing negative comps, overall, this tells us that existing items are not the problem.

How about new items?
- 2013 = $8.98.
- 2012 = $11.75.
- 2011 = $12.48.

Oh ... my ... goodness.

New items are imploding ... posting a -24% in 2013 on top of a -6% in 2012. During the past two years, new items are -28%.

This business is failing because new item productivity is failing.

Think about how hard the marketing team works to improve performance, looking under every single rock, trying to squeeze performance out of this business. All that work, all that effort, only to see that existing items are performing just fine (heck, they're actually performing better than two years ago). It's new items that are holding this business back. One of three things must be happening.
1. The rate that this company creates new "winners" is in decline.
2. This company is not investing in new merchandise.
3. This company is not investing in new merchandise, and the items this company chooses to invest in do not achieve winning status.

Later, I will explain to you why this is a catastrophe - hint - if you do not develop winning new items today, you don't have winning existing items tomorrow.

The customer is essentially telling us that s/he is starved for new merchandise, posting a -28% comp over a two year period on new merchandise.

I've run this table on more than twenty unique businesses since January 2012. Eighty percent of the time, there is a problem with merchandise productivity, and in nearly every case, new items are a much bigger problem than existing items are. For whatever the reason, the companies I work with chose to cut back on new item investments following The Great Recession. This allowed businesses to return to healthy levels of profitability faster. Today, businesses are paying for reduced new item investments. All of us make investment decisions that impact business two or three or four years out. New item / new merchandise / new product investments are among the most important a business can make. The impact of new merchandise investments are not easily tracked with the software tools we use, and therefore, are under-reported as an issue in the media.

Let's take another slice of the data, this time reviewing comp performance by channel.

Year	Freq	Phone/ Mail	Online	Email	Paid Search	Organic Search	Affiliates
2013	2	$6.05	$17.74	$5.44	$6.96	$5.91	$1.19
2012	2	$5.59	$22.17	$5.36	$7.48	$5.97	$1.63
2011	2	$5.31	$24.77	$3.98	$5.62	$5.01	$0.55

Pay close attention to the "online" column. Annual online demand is in free fall. In fact, if we compare with two years ago, we observe the following trends:

- Phone / Mail = +14%.
- Online = -28%.
- Email = +37%.
- Paid Search = +24%.
- Organic Search = +18%.
- Affiliates = +116%.
- 3rd Parties = +138%.

These metrics speak to sheer desperation on behalf of Marketing Management.

Why would I say such a thing?

- Across the industry, Phone/Mail demand has been on the decline since 1996. This tells us that Management may have been sending more catalogs out, or added pages to catalogs, trying to prop up demand.
- Online demand is in utter free fall, at a time when e-commerce is growing by 10% to 15% per year.
- Email demand is up 37%. In this case, I know that Management chose to ramp up the promotional strategy within email marketing, accounting for the increase.
- Paid and Organic Search are exhibiting healthy gains, again telling us that Marketing is trying to drive traffic through Catalogs and Email programs and Discounts/Promotions, and increased Paid Search spend.
- Affiliate comps have more than doubled - this only happens when Marketing is pushing the peanut on all available marketing channels. This only happens when customers are looking for the best possible deal.
- 3rd Party comps have more than doubled - again, Marketing is desperately trying everything possible to grow the business, leveraging an omnichannel approach.

This tells us a humbling, sad omnichannel story, doesn't it? The Marketing team is doing everything possible, leveraging all possible channels, trying so terribly hard to grow the business. And yet, customers are spending less, significantly less on new products.

In other words, the Merchandising team failed to develop new products, causing the business to implode (-28% online comp), causing Marketing to maximize all other online channels (Email, Search, Affiliates, 3rd Parties) to try to grow the business. Merchandising productivity is driving the business into the ground, Marketing is clearly reacting to these struggles by trying to maximize an omnichannel presence.

Merchandise > Omnichannel.

This problem repeats, across my client base. There are blatant merchandising problems that nobody chooses to look at. Instead, Marketing tries to prop up the business with discounts, promotions, and spend in varied and multiple channels. With poor merchandising performance, we are guaranteed to observe poor marketing ROI / ad-to-sales ratios, and this gets marketers fired. Now, there's plenty of blame to go around when it comes to bad marketers! But too often, it's merchandise productivity that is so bad that it requires the marketers to spend a fortune trying to prop up the business. Marketing investments are easily observed in the profit and loss statement. Merchandise productivity, especially from new/existing items ... well, that doesn't appear in the profit and loss statement, does it?

What have we learned, to date?
- Comp segment productivity is down 9% in the past year.
- Discounts/promotions were used to prop up performance in 2012, now with similar promo comps, the business is floundering once again.
- Existing items are +6% over the past two years - customers continue to purchase existing items.
- New items are -28% over the past two years, creating a productivity catastrophe.
- Marketing responded to the new item catastrophe (though not realizing it is a new item catastrophe - they just realize it is a catastrophe) by blowing out spend in email (via promotions), catalogs (observed via mail/phone demand), search, affiliates, and third parties.

- Marketing spend deleveraged the profit and loss statement - and that makes the CFO and CEO very, very unhappy.

This company has twenty-eight merchandise categories. Obviously, I'm not going to share what each merchandise category represents. But I will show you what the two-year trend is, in each merchandise category, for the categories generating at least 2% of annual demand:
- Category 3 = -16%.
- Category 5 = -24%.
- Category 7 = -51%.
- Category 9 = -36%.
- Category 10 = +14%
- Category 11 = -34%.
- Category 12 = +12%.
- Category 13 = +35% (large volume).
- Category 14 = -16%.
- Category 19 = -45%.
- Category 20 = +1% (large volume).
- Category 21 = +12% (large volume).
- Category 23 = -27%.
- Category 24 = +0% (large volume).
- Category 26 = -1% (large volume).
- Category 27 = +81%.

There's a story becoming apparent here. The Merchandising team decided to "double down" on high volume categories, either giving less priority to low volume categories or moving away from low volume categories altogether.
- High Volume Category Comps = +11%.
- Low Volume Category Comps = -12%.

Later in the booklet, we'll review how new/existing item productivity behaves in high volume and low volume categories.

Let's look at a couple of additional metrics. Over the past two years, demand has shifted, by month:
- January = -11%.
- February = -22%.
- March = +2%.
- April = -10%.
- May = -6%.

- June = +2%.
- July = +16%.
- August = +1%.
- September = -17%.
- October = -3%.
- November = +5%.
- <u>Cyber Monday</u> = +74%.
- December = -6%.

We can revise the figures a bit:
- January - October = -5%.
- November - December = +3%.

The analysis showed that, in November, and on Cyber Monday in particular, customers were given increased discounts and promotions, giving customers enhanced opportunities to buy during these timeframes. And customers obliged! Imagine that? In fact, Cyber Monday demand is +74% over the past two years, a timeframe when the business did not exhibit growth.

This is so important, folks. When a business shifts to a discount-centric model, demand pours out of some timeframes (January - October in this case), into other timeframes (Christmas in this case ... and Cyber Monday in particular). This business is just moving deck chairs around on the Titanic, moving demand out of full-price timeframes into promotional Christmas / Cyber Monday windows. This will cause Christmas-centric merchandise to appear to perform better, causing Spring/Summer merchandise to appear to perform worse. Merchants will respond to this by emphasizing buys for Christmas / Cyber Monday, de-emphasizing buys for Spring/Summer.

Stated differently:
- New items perform poorly.
- Marketing responds by increasing promotions.
- Increased promotions shift demand out of Jan-Oct, into Christmas and Cyber Monday.
- Merchandise in the Christmas / Cyber Monday window performs better due to the discounts, causing the merchandising team to emphasize the Christmas merchandise assortment.

It doesn't have to be this way, folks!

This business would be better served to address the new merchandise productivity issue than to use marketing promotions to re-shape the structure of the business.

Let's look at one last view of the data, using this methodology. Here, we look at comps by price point, comparing 2013 to 2011:
- $0.01 to $9.99 Items = -10%.
- $10.00 to $19.99 Items = -8%.
- $20.00 to $29.99 Items = -8%.
- $30.00 to $49.99 Items = +3%.
- $50.00 or Greater Items = +3%.

The data shows us that Management is emphasizing more expensive items, in an attempt to grow top-line demand. Repeatedly, we observe Management making a series of interesting strategic choices to prop up the business, ignoring the core issue illustrated by this analysis ... an implosion of new item productivity.

Class of Reporting

The comp segment analysis made it clear that there is a significant, dramatic new merchandise issue. We can use a "Class of" style report to begin to understand the issues surrounding merchandise.

Here's what we will do. We identify the first year that an item was introduced into the merchandising assortment. Let's pretend that year is 2008. This item becomes part of the "Class of" 2008. We follow the performance of this item, and all items, through the current year (2013). We want to see how those items perform/decay over time.

For the business we're analyzing, here's what the table looks like:

Class Of	New Items	2011 Demand	2012 Demand	2013 Demand
2011 Items	383	$6,941,432	$7,412,444	$4,346,890
2012 Items	320	$0	$5,947,087	$4,977,865
2013 Items	291	$0	$0	$4,692,037
Total Demand		$25,989,908	$25,905,127	$22,814,491
% From New		27%	23%	21%

Recall earlier in the booklet, we discussed how comp segment demand from new items was on the decline:
- 2011 = $12.48.
- 2012 = $11.75.
- 2013 = $8.48.

Now look at the number of new items, introduced by year:
- 2011 = 383 new items.
- 2012 = 320 new items.
- 2013 = 291 new items.

Oh boy.

And look at demand for new items in the year the new item was introduced:
- 2011 = $6,941,432 demand - 383 new items - $18,123 per item.
- 2012 = $5,947,087 demand - 320 new items - $18,585 per item.
- 2013 = $4,692,037 demand - 291 new items - $16,124 per item.

Finally, look at the percentage of total demand generated by new items.
- 2011 = 27%.
- 2012 = 23%.
- 2013 = 21%.

It becomes clear that the drop off in comp segment performance on new items is due to two reasons.
- 2012: A reduction in the number of new items.
- 2013: A reduction in the number of new items, and a significant drop in productivity per new item.

Notice that demand dropped from $6.9 million in new items in 2011 to $4.7 million from new items in 2013, a decrease of $2.2 million. The total business declined by $3.1 million during that timeframe.

In other words, merchandising decisions regarding new items are responsible for 71% of the total demand drop over the past two years.

Wow.

I know, I know, you're a marketer, you're going to say that the drop is a lot more complicated than this. Of course the drop in demand is more complicated than this. But what do you think the confidence interval is around my estimate? Say it is +/- 20 percentage points ... meaning that new items are responsible for between 51% and 91% of the demand drop. So what?

In other words, it doesn't matter how close the estimate is to being perfectly accurate - this is the issue. It's sitting there, in plain sight. This business did not invest in new merchandise. This business, as a result, is suffering, it is not growing, it is shrinking.

As I mentioned earlier in the booklet, I found that 80% of the businesses I put through the Merchandise Forensics framework had merchandising issues, mostly new merchandise issues. Sure, there were marketing challenges, but they didn't account for more than a hiccup or two compared to the merchandising issues I found.

Do you think there might be merchandise issues in your business?

Wouldn't you want to identify the issues?

Let's go back to the table. Look at the "Class of 2011". Those items generated $6.9 million the first year, then generated $7.4 million in 2012, and finally, $4.3 million in 2013. This is a critical finding, one that I find in nearly every project I work on.

This concept is called "decay".

In other words, items that perform well eventually find their peak, they plateau, then they begin to decay, eventually being replaced by new merchandise. We will revisit the concept of "decay" shortly.

Item Grades

In every Merchandise Forensics project, I grade items based on annual demand/unit volume. I analyze every item that generated at least $0.01 demand in the past twelve months, breaking annual demand and units into one-percentile groups.

Next, I determine three sets of criteria.

1. Cutoff for the top 5% of item demand.
2. Cutoff for the top 5% of unit volume.
3. Cutoff for the top 45% of demand volume.

This allows me to create a segmentation strategy.
- A = Item in top 5% of demand volume, and in top 5% of unit volume.
- B = Item in top 5% of demand volume only.
- C = Item in top 5% of unit volume only.
- D = Item not in top 5%, but is in top 45% of demand volume.
- F = All remaining items.

"A" items are critically important. These items carry the weight of the business on their shoulders. "A" items frequently account for 30% of the total annual sales volume. Every employee should intuitively know which items are "A" items.

"B" items are expensive items, items that do not generate high unit volume, but by virtue of a high price point, comprise a significant amount of annual demand. Still, these items account for 20% of annual demand volume.

"C" items are low-price items that generate high unit volume, but do not generate a ton of demand. "C" items are important because so many customers purchase them.

"D" items represent items that serve a niche purpose, or are in transition. "D" items are frequently items that are ascending in importance, or are gently heading toward being retired.

"F" items are mostly unimportant, unless the quantity of "F" items increase as a rate proportional to A/B/C/D item decreases. These are items that are no longer actively sold, but generate a small amount of volume, or are simply items that customers, for the most part, do not want to purchase.

Let's look at a series of grading tables for our business, for the past three years. For this business, we have our three key cutoffs.
- 5% Demand Cutoff = $88,000 per year.
- 5% Item Cutoff = 3,350 items per year.
- 45% Demand Cutoff = $4,100 per year.

This gives us five grades:

- A = At least $88,000 demand and 3,350 units sold.
- B = At least $88,000 demand, < 3,350 units sold.
- C = Less than $88,000 demand, > 3,350 units sold.
- D = Not in A/B/C, at least $4,100 demand last year.
- F = $0.01 to $4,100 demand last year.

Here's how demand and units distribute for our business, for the past three years:

Grade	Demand	Units	Price
A	$6,784,635	267,934	$25.32
B	$4,723,595	47,409	$99.64
C	$1,594,426	160,841	$9.91
D	$8,918,897	370,874	$24.05
F	$792,939	54,402	$14.58
Totals	$22,814,491	901,458	$25.31

A/B/C items represent a whopping 57% of total annual demand, and 53% of annual unit volume. "D" items represent 39% of total annual demand and 41% of total annual unit volume. "F" items don't generate a material amount of volume, 3% of demand and 6% of unit volume.

Now, let's take a peek at the number of items in each grade. Here's the table:

	2013	2012	2011
A	32	35	38
B	31	34	33
C	31	36	49
D	465	534	497
F	683	634	637
Totals	1,242	1,273	1,254
A-C Tots.	94	105	120

This table can be misleading, can't it?

This business had 1,254 items generating at least a penny of demand in 2011, then 1,273 items in 2012, and 1,242 items in 2013.

So there isn't an item issue, in total.

But there are issues with "A", "B", and "C" items.
- "A" items, generating top 5% levels in both demand and units, the most important items of all, have declined from 38 to 35 to 32 ... a drop of nearly 20% in just two years.
- "B" items are somewhat constant - from 33 to 34 and then down to 31 in the past year. Remember, "B" items are high demand, high price point, low unit items. Earlier, we observed that Management appeared to be pushing more expensive items. This row in the table partially confirms our observation.
- "C" items are high unit / lower demand volume items. We see these items in free fall, from 49 to 36 to 31 in 2013. It looks like Management is de-emphasizing high unit volume, low price point items.
- "D" items are down, too, though they rose a bit in 2012, probably propping demand up just a bit in 2012.

So the best items (A/B/C) all dropped, with Bs holding closest to steady. But we would expect that to happen in a business that we demonstrated earlier to be struggling quite a bit, right? And we noticed that average order values increased consistently, a fact verified by the flat number of "B" items and the decline in "C" items.

Let's look at how these items distribute, by new and existing. This should be telling, folks:

Totals	2013	2012	2011
A	32	35	38
B	31	34	33
C	31	36	49
D	465	534	497
F	683	634	637
Totals	1,242	1,273	1,254
A-C Tots.	94	105	120

Existing	2013	2012	2011
A	27	28	29
B	25	29	26
C	24	27	36
D	353	379	332
F	522	491	449
Totals	951	954	872
A-C Tots.	76	84	91

New	2013	2012	2011
A	5	7	9
B	6	5	7
C	7	9	13
D	112	155	165
F	161	143	188
Totals	291	319	382
A-C Tots.	18	21	29

Basically, this is a business that is imploding. Simply imploding. But the business is imploding faster among new items than among existing items.

During the past two years:
- Existing A/B/C items decreased by 16%.
- New A/B/C items decreased by 38%.

New, winning items are pulling our business down into the muck!

Revisiting Decay

Earlier, I discussed how items tend to "decay" over time. We can demonstrate this by analyzing how A/B/C/D/F items from 2012 performed in 2013.

There are two tables I use to perform this analysis. The first table looks at how last year's A/B/C/D/F items are graded at the end of this year.

2012 Grade	2012 Items	2013 Grade = A	2013 Grade = B	2013 Grade = C	2013 Grade = D	2013 Grade = F	2013 Not Avail.
A	35	20	2	4	4	3	2
B	34	1	17	0	12	2	2
C	36	0	0	14	18	3	1
D	534	4	2	5	277	170	76
F	634	2	4	1	42	344	241
New	291	5	6	7	112	161	0

Read across the "A" row. There were 35 items earning a grade of "A" in 2012. Of that total, only 20 (57%) stay at an "A" level. That's a terribly important finding, folks. It means that "A" items do not stay at an "A" level, they decay over time - in fact, they decay significantly within just twelve months! This means that we have to get new "A" items from other grades, or the business implodes.

"A" items degrade fairly evenly, with 2 becoming a "B", 4 becoming a "C", 4 becoming a "D", and 3 becoming an "F". Heck, only 2 items were not carried over (that's a good thing - you want to see your best items carried over from one year to another).

Look at "B" items. These items are unlikely to upgrade. Just 1 of 34 move up to "A" status, while a whopping 12 of 34 drop down to "D" status. We cannot count on "B" items (high demand, low items) to maintain their lofty status either, they degrade quickly.

Look at "C" items. These items are unlikely to upgrade. Zero of 36 move up to "A" status, 14 hold their own, while a whopping 18 drop down to "D" status. We cannot count on "C" items (low demand, high item count) to maintain their lofty status, they also degrade quickly.

"D" items have no chance, do they? Just 4 of 534 graduate to "A" status, just 2 of 534 graduate to "B" status, just 5 of 534 move up to "C" status.

Meanwhile, 177 "D" items fall down to "F" status, and 76 are fully discontinued.

Now look at "F" items. Only 2 of 634 graduate to "A" status, 4 of 634 graduate to "B" status, just 1 of 634 moves up to "C" status. Only 42 of 634 bother to improve to "D" status.

This is so important, folks.

This doesn't only happen in this one example. This happens in every single project I work on. Merchandise Forensics indicate that very few items become best sellers. Items simply do not graduate to high productivity status, items achieve their potential quickly, then begin their slow decay.

The only way to combat this, then, is to have a fully developed new item graduation program. We simply must set goals for our merchandising partners - there must be "x" new items, and of the "x" new items, a certain fraction must achieve a grade of "A", "B", or "C". It's really the only solution to this problem.

In our case, Management decided to de-emphasize new item development, the exact opposite strategy that our findings require of us. This only accelerates the drop off in business performance.

Can you see that these problems are merchandise driven? Can you see that your typical analytics package makes it nearly impossible for you to visualize or identify this problem?

Here's one more view of decay. Let's look at each grade, for the items that were carried over from one year to the next, measuring the percentage of demand that also carries over.

2012 Grade	2012 Demand	2013 Demand	Demand Retained	Decay Rate
A	$7,067,054	$5,506,803	77.9%	22.1%
B	$4,749,089	$3,085,540	65.0%	35.0%
C	$1,760,582	$1,091,572	62.0%	38.0%
D	$9,416,349	$6,173,031	65.6%	34.4%
F	$534,706	$2,158,018	403.6%	n/a
Totals	$23,527,780	$18,014,964	76.6%	23.4%

Well, isn't that telling?

"A" items decay at a 22% rate.

"B" items decay at a 35% rate.

"C" items decay at a 38% rate.

"D" items decay at a 34% rate.

"F" items actually pick up ground.

Overall, the decay rate is 23%.

These results are pretty typical. To be honest, for healthy companies, you subtract about 8% from the decay rates above - "A" items would decay at 14% instead of 22%, the overall rate might be 15% instead of 23%.

Again, this information proves my point. We simply must have a robust new item development program to offset the concept of decay. We cannot let our merchandise become stale.

Merchandise decay is common, across every project I work on.

New item development varies, however. Some companies make this a priority, others don't. Consistently, the companies that experience success have robust new item development programs.

Grades by Merchandise Category

Earlier, I discussed the fact that there were five categories (13, 20, 21, 24, and 26) that were high-volume categories. These categories experienced comp segment demand increases, whereas all other categories experienced comp segment demand decreases.

Let's look at grades, new and existing, for the high volume categories.

Totals	2013	2012	2011
A	16	16	18
B	17	18	13
C	14	15	16
D	174	203	183
F	199	183	164
Totals	420	435	394
A-C Tots.	47	49	47

Existing	2013	2012	2011
A	12	11	12
B	12	14	9
C	9	10	10
D	123	121	101
F	148	128	112
Totals	304	284	244
A-C Tots.	33	35	31

New	2013	2012	2011
A	4	5	6
B	5	4	4
C	5	5	6
D	51	82	82
F	51	55	52
Totals	116	151	150
A-C Tots.	14	14	16

Well, isn't this interesting?

Existing A/B/C items are holding steady. New A/B/C items are mostly steady, though the total number of new "D" items dropped significantly. Still, the story here isn't terribly dire. The high volume categories have been managed reasonably well. Comp segment customer performance is positive among these categories.

If that is the case, then the story for all other categories must not be quite as optimistic. Let's take a look:

Totals	2013	2012	2011
A	16	19	20
B	14	16	20
C	17	21	33
D	291	331	314
F	484	451	473
Totals	822	838	860
A-C Tots.	47	56	73

Existing	2013	2012	2011
A	15	17	17
B	13	15	17
C	15	17	26
D	230	258	231
F	374	363	337
Totals	647	670	628
A-C Tots.	43	49	60

New	2013	2012	2011
A	1	2	3
B	1	1	3
C	2	4	7
D	61	73	83
F	110	88	136
Totals	175	168	232
A-C Tots.	4	7	13

Oh boy.

What do you observe, here? Well, existing A/B/C items are down 29% over the past two years, mostly from "C" items. This means that Management likely discontinued several low-demand, high-unit items.

New items, well, that's where the story spirals out of control. There were 13 new A/B/C items in these categories two years ago, there are just 4 today, a reduction of 69%. The number of new "D" items is down, significantly, as well.

The data suggest that Management is focusing all efforts on high-volume categories. Customers responded appropriately, actually spending more in high-volume categories over a two-year period of time.

The data suggest that Management is phasing out, or is not emphasizing low-volume categories. Not surprisingly, customers are spending less in those categories. And because customers are spending less in these categories, Marketing ramped-up discounts and promotions, trying to recover business across the rest of the brand. The increase in discounts and promotions moved business out of January - October, into November, and especially into Cyber Monday, a strong promotional holiday where margins are not great.

Do you see how Merchandise Forensics help illustrate how decisions among Merchants lead to Marketing decisions that spiral the business into great difficulty? The merchandising team de-emphasized low-volume categories, and in particular, stopped cultivating outstanding new items in low-volume categories. Customers responded by spending dramatically less across new items, largely fueled by the cutback in low-volume categories. Marketing responded by increasing discounts/promotions to fuel demand missing because of strategic merchandising decisions. Marketing also responded by exploding spend in other marketing channels (email, search, affiliates, 3rd parties), trying desperately to grow the business, given the shortcomings in merchandise productivity.

This business is failing because of merchandising issues. Merchandise Forensics allow us to identify the merchandising issues.

Sales Differences by Channel

In many projects, there are significant differences in merchandise sales by channel. In the case I am going to present to you, that's not true.

Here's percentage of demand for existing customers, by marketing channel.

Existing Customers	New Items	Existing Items	Grade = A	Grade = B	Grade = C	Grade = D	Grade = F
Phone / Mail	24.3%	75.7%	25.1%	22.0%	7.6%	42.3%	3.0%
Online	20.8%	79.2%	30.6%	18.1%	8.6%	39.1%	3.6%
Email	22.0%	78.0%	27.5%	15.8%	8.1%	43.2%	5.4%
Paid Search	19.8%	80.2%	31.2%	20.2%	7.8%	37.4%	3.4%
Organic Search	19.7%	80.3%	30.6%	18.8%	8.0%	38.9%	3.7%
Affiliates	21.4%	78.6%	29.4%	20.0%	7.9%	38.9%	3.8%
3rd Parties	18.1%	81.9%	39.1%	16.7%	5.0%	38.0%	1.1%

The differences are subtle, not major. Phone/Mail customers do skew a bit to new items, suggesting that catalog marketing efforts provide a marketing vehicle to educate the customer about new merchandise. Conversely, search and third parties are calibrated just a bit more to existing items, suggesting that customers are looking for time-honored favorites (or that those items are more likely to be featured in search activities).

Search and third parties skew more heavily to Grade "A" items as well. In this case, I don't know if landing pages are calibrated to best sellers, or the most popular keywords align with best sellers.

Finally, email skews a bit to "F" items. Email is a place where you can feature obscure items, hoping to generate a sales bump among those items, given that there is almost no variable cost associated with email marketing.

Here's the same table, for first-time buyers:

New Customers	New Items	Existing Items	Grade = A	Grade = B	Grade = C	Grade = D	Grade = F
Phone / Mail	23.4%	76.6%	27.7%	25.1%	5.9%	39.6%	1.7%
Online	20.9%	79.1%	28.6%	22.3%	6.4%	39.0%	3.7%
Email	23.7%	76.3%	26.1%	16.5%	7.0%	45.2%	5.3%
Paid Search	19.3%	80.7%	29.1%	25.3%	5.6%	36.6%	3.5%
Organic Search	17.9%	82.1%	29.5%	21.5%	6.2%	38.8%	4.0%
Affiliates	22.1%	77.9%	29.0%	23.5%	6.2%	37.5%	3.8%
3rd Parties	17.7%	82.3%	39.8%	15.5%	4.8%	38.6%	1.4%

In this case, the numbers are directionally similar, so there's not much to talk about. In many projects, however, new customers have a very clear merchandise preference, one that is substantially different from the preferences of existing customers.

Repurchase Rates by Price Point

Earlier in the booklet, we noticed that Management was de-emphasizing low price point items, apparently promoting high price point items to generate demand.

Low price point items play an important role in any business. Low price points cause customers to add-on to orders. Low price points cause more customers to purchase. Generally speaking, I would prefer to have two customers buying $20 items than to have one customer purchasing a $40 item, as long as the gross margins are identical.

The following table illustrates how annual customer repurchase rates vary by price point and grade.

Price Point	Grade	2012 Items	2013 Reb. Rate
$1 to $10	A	5	37.1%
	B	0	n/a
	C	17	36.0%
	D	83	36.1%
	F	192	32.4%
$10 to $19	A	12	33.7%
	B	0	n/a
	C	19	35.4%
	D	156	34.6%
	F	198	33.3%
$20 to $29	A	6	34.7%
	B	1	38.5%
	C	1	40.1%
	D	95	32.6%
	F	92	27.4%
$30 to $49	A	8	32.0%
	B	6	31.6%
	C	0	n/a
	D	93	29.9%
	F	64	29.9%
$50 and up	A	5	31.2%
	B	28	28.0%
	C	0	n/a
	D	108	29.2%
	F	89	29.1%

What do we observe in this table? First, annual repurchase rates for customers buying expensive items are lower, on average, than are repurchase rates for customers buying inexpensive items. Low price point items do, for this business, increase annual customer repurchase rates. Remember, we discovered that Management was de-emphasizing inexpensive price points. This means that Management was, inadvertently driving down annual repurchase rates. That's not a wise decision, is it?

The table above can be summarized by price point, and by grade.

By Price Point:
- $0.01 to $9.99 = 33.7% customer repurchase rate.
- $10.00 to $19.99 = 33.9% customer repurchase rate.
- $20.00 to $29.99 = 30.3% customer repurchase rate.
- $30.00 to $49.99 = 30.1% customer repurchase rate.
- $50.00 and up = 29.1% customer repurchase rate.

By Grade:
- Grade A = 33.6% customer repurchase rate.
- Grade B = 28.8% customer repurchase rate.
- Grade C = 35.8% customer repurchase rate.
- Grade D = 32.6% customer repurchase rate.
- Grade F = 31.3% customer repurchase rate.

Yes, for this business, price points do matter. This is the case across most of my projects, as well. Merchandise in low price point bands causes customers to come back and repurchase at higher rates than does merchandise in high price point ranges.

This is validated in the "By Grade" table. Remember, "B" items are items that generate high sales volumes on low unit totals (i.e. expensive items). This grade yields low customer repurchase rates.

It appears that Management tried to de-emphasize lower price point items. This decision harms subsequent customer repurchase rates.

We can also look at repurchase rates for customers buying new items, comparing them to repurchase rates for customers buying existing items.

Here's the data for our business.
- Existing Items = 31.4% repurchase rate.
- New Items = 33.7% repurchase rate.

For this business, customers who buy new items have a greater future repurchase rate than do customers buying existing items. This suggests that new items are an important way to keep customers coming back. Recall that Management de-emphasized new items in low-volume categories. This is another unintentional mistake that is hurting the business.

A word of caution. It is important to control for past purchase activity. If you find that customers buying existing items are of fundamentally lower quality than are customers buying new items, then you need to make an adjustment, based on prior buying activity, before reporting figures to Management.

Loyalty Killers

In the dataset analyzed for this project, there were 35 items that earned a grade of "A". However, these items were not created equally.
- 6 items yielded customers with a 40% or greater repurchase rate.
- 19 items yielded customers with a 30% to 39.9% repurchase rate.
- 9 items yielded customers with a 25% to a 29.9% repurchase rate.
- 1 item yielded customers with a 21% annual repurchase rate.

In other words, there are 10 items that earned a grade of "A" in 2012, but then caused customers to repurchase at low rates in 2013.

These items are called "Loyalty Killers". These items have an attribute associated with them that cause customers to purchase less frequently in the future. Maybe the item is only sold at Christmas, and therefore, does not drive repurchase during January - October. Maybe the item has a long repurchase cycle. Maybe the item simply fills a customer need, admirably! Maybe the item is of poor quality, and angers the customer. Regardless, loyalty killers should not featured at the front of a catalog, and should not be featured in email marketing campaigns.

The Merchandise Forensics Map

Sometimes, the number of attributes we analyze become overwhelming. Sometimes, we simply need a visualization of customer behavior, especially when it comes to how customers interact with merchandise and channels.

If you don't like geeky math, I invite you to page ahead to the forthcoming map. Otherwise, here's my methodology for creating a Merchandise Forensics Map.

Step 1 = Identify Weights. I run a regression model to learn how important historical transactions are, compared to current transactions, using twelve month future demand as the dependent variable, and twelve-month historical variables (0-12, 13-24, 25-36, 37-48, 49-60, 61+) as independent variables. I only run the model on 0-12 month buyers. For the table I will illustrate later, the weights are 1.00 for 0-12 month purchases, 0.50 for 13-24 month purchases, 0.30 for 25-36 month purchases, 0.20 for 37-48 month purchases, 0.15 for 49-60 month purchases, 0.12 for 61-72 month purchases, and 0.10 for 73+ month purchases. For instance, if a customer spends $100 0-12 months ago, and spends $100 37-48 months ago, weighted historical demand is $100*1.00 + $100*0.20 = $120.

Step 2 = Create Weighted Variables. I create weighted historical variables for each advertising/marketing channel (catalog, email, online, search, that kind of thing), each merchandising category, each month (including a separate variable for Cyber Monday), each price point category (0-10, 10-20, 20-30, 30-50, 50+), for transactions tied to a marketing promotion, and for transactions tied to a first purchase.

Step 3 = Select 12 Month Buyers.

Step 4 = Compute Weighted Percentages. Say a customer spent $120 on weighted email transactions, and spent a total of $200 weighted historical dollars. Weighted email transactions = $120 / $200 = 0.60.

Step 5 = Run A Factor Analysis. For me, this is fun! I analyze the weighted percentage variables (channels, categories, months, price points, new buyers, loyal buyers, promotions). I only extract two factors, using varimax rotation. I save each of the two calculated factors as new variables.

Step 6 = Segment Each Factor. For each factor, I create three categorical values ... 1 = a value < -0.40 ... 2 = a value between -0.40 and 0.40 ... 3 = a value > 0.40.

Step 7 = Create Map Segments. I calculate Segment1 * 10 + Segment2 = Nine Segments. The values are 11 (Lower Left), 12 (Middle Left), 13 (Upper Left), 21 (Lower Middle), 22 (Middle Middle), 23 (Upper Middle), 31 (Lower Right), 32 (Middle Right), and 33 (Upper Right).

Step 8 = Calculate average weighted percentages by Map Segment (11, 12, 13, 21, 22, 23, 31, 32, 33).

Step 9 = Label each cell in the Map, where average weighted percentages are valued well above the overall average. In other words, if the average amount of January demand is 8% of total weighted demand, and three cells have 10%, 15%, and 20%, then in those cells, we label them with a "January" label.

Step 10 = Print the Map.

Ok, let's take a look at the map representing the business in our case study.

New Buyers	Online	Loyal Buyers, Promotions
Organic Search, 3rd Parties	Online	Online, Email, Affiliates
Categories 01, 02, 03, 04, 05, 07, 10, 15, 22, 24, 26, 27	Categories 07, 09, 10, 12, 15, 19, 24, 26, 27	Categories 09, 12, 19, 24, 26
Feb, Mar, Apr, May, Jun, Jul, Aug	Mar, Apr, May, Jun, Jul, Aug	Mar, Apr, May, Jun, Jul, Aug
$10.00 - $19.99	$10.00 - $19.99	$50.00+
New Buyers	Paid Search	Loyal Buyers, Promotions
Organic Search, 3rd Party	Paid Search	Email, Paid Search, Affiliates
Categories 04, 05, 06, 07, 23, 25, 28	Categories 07, 12, 14, 17, 18, 20, 23	Categories 09, 11, 12, 14, 20, 23
Aug, Sep, Oct	Jan, Feb, Aug, Sep	Jan, Feb, Mar, Apr, Aug, Sep
$10.00 - $19.99	$30.00 - $49.99	$50.00+
New Buyers	Phone, Paid Search	Loyal Buyers, Promotions
Phone, 3rd Party	Phone, Paid Search	Phone, Email, Paid Search, Affiliates
Categories 06, 13, 16	Categories 08, 13, 18, 21	Categories 08, 11, 13, 14, 21
Oct, Nov, Cyber Monday, Dec	Nov, Cyber Monday, Dec	Nov, Cyber Monday, Dec
$20.00 - $29.99	$30.00 - $49.99	$50.00+

Each cell in this table represents customer commonality. Let's take a look at the lower left cell. This cell is represented by New Buyers, Phone Transactions, 3rd Party Transactions (like Amazon, for instance), Merchandise Categories 6/13/16. Furthermore, we observe October, November, Cyber Monday, and December transactions. Finally, price points between $20.00 and $29.99 are preferred.

The story of this business is illustrated in this image.

Look at the right hand side of this Merchandise Forensics Map. Here we find loyal customers, promotions, and high price points. Management is clearly marketing discounts and promotions to the most loyal customers, and loyal customers respond by buying expensive items at a discount. Think about this for a moment. We learned earlier that Management was de-emphasizing low price point items. Well, customers listened. The most loyal customers purchased, buying expensive items with discounts/promotions, defeating the purpose of increasing AOV and margin by selling more expensive items.

Look at the bottom row. This is the Christmas season, featuring Category 13. New customers buy at low price points, loyal buyers buy at high price points after applying discounts/promotions.

Notice that email is consistently aligned with loyal buyers, consistently aligned with discounts/promotions. I see this happen all the time. Email has been compromised, becoming the go-to channel for customers looking to get the best deal. Also notice that Affiliates are consistently aligned with promotions, again, suggesting that Affiliates align with customers looking for the best possible deal.

Notice that paid search is not aligned with new customers, but is aligned with best customers.

Notice that organic search is aligned with new customers in summer months, suggesting that catalogs are creating demand that organic search is fulfilling (given that this is a catalog brand that does extensive catalog marketing in the summer months).

The map allows us to align merchandise categories with timeframes and channels. Organic search, for instance, aligns with categories 4, 5, and 7. These are key categories that can be merchandised in landing page strategies. Category 14 aligns with paid search.

I use this structure to explain to Executives the customer/merchandising ecosystem. In one image, we get to see how merchandise categories, marketing channel, promotions, price points, seasons, and customer loyalty all fit together. There are few other methods that achieve this objective.

Average Item Age

Periodically, my projects suggest that there is an interaction between the channels a customer purchases from, and the items a customer purchases. Here's the table for our business.

Channel	Avg. Item Age
Phone/Mail	2.63
Online	2.68
Email	2.63
Paid Search	2.75
Organic Search	2.75
Affiliates	2.69
3rd Party	2.81

In our case, there are no significant differences in the number of years an item has been offered, by channel.

When I work with catalog brands, it is common to see the phone/mail channel aligned with items that are "old" - meaning that existing old-school customers buy traditional winners.

This creates a problem for most businesses. When long-time buyers keep buying the same items through the same channels, over and over again, the merchandising team gets caught in a trap. Merchants look at reports, and learn that they need to keep buying the stuff they've always purchased. Ultimately, the business ages, it accelerates toward an older customer base, becoming cutoff from mainstream customer demographics.

Over the next few years, pay close attention to what customers are purchasing in your mobile channel. You're likely to see different merchandise aligning with the mobile channel than with traditional channels.

Where Is This Business Headed?

We seldom get to observe the long-term impact of today's merchandising strategies, do we?

We can, however, simulate what might happen. For our case study, assuming we continue the same new item strategy currently employed, we're likely to witness this outcome:

Merchandise Forensics Forecast

Items	Last Year	Today	After Year 1	After Year 2	After Year 3	After Year 4	After Year 5
Existing A	35	32	30	29	28	27	26
Existing B	34	31	29	27	27	26	25
Existing C	36	31	28	26	25	24	24
Existing D	534	462	423	400	385	376	370
Existing F	634	671	667	653	638	625	615
New A		5	5	5	5	5	5
New B		6	6	6	6	6	6
New C		7	7	7	7	7	7
New D		112	112	112	112	112	112
New F		161	161	161	161	161	161
Demand (in 000s)		$22,775	$21,155	$20,094	$19,368	$18,856	$18,492

That's not a favorable outcome, is it? If we keep on fueling the business with too-few highly productive new items, well, we drive the business down by about 5% per year, every year. Look at how A/B/C items are starved, over time, dropping down to 75 total in five years, down from 94 today.

That's not what we want to see happen, is it?

So let's try something. Let's increase all new items by 20%. Here's the outcome of the simulation:

Merchandise Forensics Forecast

Items	Last Year	Today	After Year 1	After Year 2	After Year 3	After Year 4	After Year 5
Existing A	35	32	31	31	30	30	30
Existing B	34	31	30	30	29	29	29
Existing C	36	31	29	28	28	27	27
Existing D	534	462	445	437	433	430	429
Existing F	634	671	700	709	712	712	711
New A		5	6	6	6	6	6
New B		6	7	7	7	7	7
New C		7	8	8	8	8	8
New D		112	134	134	134	134	134
New F		161	193	193	193	193	193
Demand (in 000s)		$22,775	$22,089	$21,709	$21,489	$21,354	$21,266

My goodness, that's not enough to grow the business! We need an even larger infusion of new items.

Merchandise Forensics Forecast

Items	Last Year	Today	After Year 1	After Year 2	After Year 3	After Year 4	After Year 5
Existing A	35	32	34	36	38	39	41
Existing B	34	31	33	36	38	39	41
Existing C	36	31	33	35	36	37	38
Existing D	534	462	512	549	575	593	606
Existing F	634	671	796	879	934	972	999
New A		5	9	9	9	9	9
New B		6	11	11	11	11	11
New C		7	13	13	13	13	13
New D		112	202	202	202	202	202
New F		161	290	290	290	290	290
Demand (in 000s)		$22,775	$24,893	$26,552	$27,853	$28,846	$29,591

This example featured an 80% increase in new items. Eighty percent! That's what it takes to stimulate enough demand to move this business forward by between 10% and 20% per year.

The simulation shows that this business must cultivate 9 "A" items, 11 "B" items, and 13 "C" items per year, in order to have a chance to grow at an acceptable rate.

Let's do a test - we'll hold D/F items constant, and only increase A/B/C new items.

Merchandise Forensics Forecast

Items	Last Year	Today	After Year 1	After Year 2	After Year 3	After Year 4	After Year 5
Existing A	35	32	34	35	36	36	36
Existing B	34	31	33	35	35	35	35
Existing C	36	31	33	34	34	34	34
Existing D	534	462	423	405	395	390	387
Existing F	634	671	667	654	641	632	625
New A		5	9	9	9	9	9
New B		6	11	11	11	11	11
New C		7	13	13	13	13	13
New D		112	112	112	112	112	112
New F		161	161	161	161	161	161
Demand (in 000s)		$22,775	$22,945	$23,128	$23,172	$23,149	$23,102

The business still grows, though not much.

Now we'll do the opposite - we'll hold A/B/C items constant, growing new D/F items by 80% a year.

Merchandise Forensics Forecast

Items	Last Year	Today	After Year 1	After Year 2	After Year 3	After Year 4	After Year 5
Existing A	35	32	30	30	30	30	31
Existing B	34	31	29	29	29	30	31
Existing C	36	31	28	27	27	27	27
Existing D	534	462	512	544	565	579	589
Existing F	634	671	796	878	931	965	988
New A		5	5	5	5	5	5
New B		6	6	6	6	6	6
New C		7	7	7	7	7	7
New D		112	202	202	202	202	202
New F		161	290	290	290	290	290
Demand (in 000s)		$22,775	$23,103	$23,518	$24,049	$24,553	$24,981

The business grows at the same, tepid rate, doesn't it.

In other words, new item development (not just winners, but all items) is critically important to the success of this business.

Merchandise Improvements May Not Be Linear

In some cases, I've analyzed businesses where an increase in new items does not yield a proportional increase in demand.

In other words, if you increase the new item assortment by 80%, you disproportionately push items into D/F categories, you do not increase A/B/C items by 80%. Therefore, in your forecasting, you may wish to be conservative in the assignment of A/B/C items. Your forecast might look something like this:

Merchandise Forensics Forecast

Items	Last Year	Today	After Year 1	After Year 2	After Year 3	After Year 4	After Year 5
Existing A	35	32	32	33	34	35	36
Existing B	34	31	31	32	34	35	36
Existing C	36	31	30	31	32	32	33
Existing D	534	462	512	547	571	588	600
Existing F	634	671	806	894	951	989	1,015
New A		5	7	7	7	7	7
New B		6	8	8	8	8	8
New C		7	10	10	10	10	10
New D		112	202	202	202	202	202
New F		161	300	300	300	300	300
Demand (in 000s)		$22,775	$24,008	$25,080	$26,033	$26,814	$27,426

Notice that the business is still forecast to grow at a healthy rate, but our A/B/C items only grow by 40%, not 80%. Be conservative, in order to hedge your bets against the possibility that demand does not increase linearly when you add a glut of new items to the assortment.

What Have We Learned?

Pretend this is your business. What did a Merchandise Forensics project teach you?

Finding #1: This business is really, really struggling to generate demand. But we already knew that, simply by looking at annual demand for the past three years.

Finding #2: It was obvious that business was struggling in 2012, even though demand held steady and comp segment performance improved. During the year, Management elected to ramp up discounts and promotions, in an effort to prop up demand.

Finding #3: With promotions comp'd from 2012 to 2013, there was nothing new to prop up demand. As a result, demand crumbled.

Finding #4: Marketing responded to this challenge by greatly expanding the catalog marketing program, search marketing program, affiliate marketing program, 3rd party marketing program, and email marketing program. Marketing "bought" demand with discounts/promotions in 2012. Marketing "bought" demand with discounts/promotions/ad-dollars in 2013.

Finding #5: A comp segment analysis suggested that customers are continuing to buy existing items at acceptable levels, +6% from 2011 to 2013.

Finding #6: A comp segment analysis suggested that customers are buying dramatically fewer new items in 2013 (-28%), compared to 2011. This drop in customer productivity is responsible for a drop in comp segment performance over the past two years. This is the reason the business is struggling, folks.

Finding #7: Comps are generally down in most seasons - but are up significantly on Cyber Monday. This business is clearly buying gains via discounts and promotions.

Finding #8: High volume merchandising categories are exhibiting positive comps. Low volume merchandising categories are exhibiting negative comps. The merchandising team is clearly de-emphasizing low volume categories, to the detriment of comp segment performance.

Finding #9: Comp segment performance is down significantly among low priced items. Comp segment performance is up marginally among high priced items. The merchandising team clearly de-emphasized low price items, likely in an effort to boost demand through high priced items. This strategy did not work.

Finding #10: Not surprisingly, the merchandising team cut way back on the number of new items offered in 2012, and again in 2013. Worse, productivity of new items in 2013 dropped significantly. This combination of decisions caused customers to continue to spend money on existing items, but not increase spend among new items, significantly hurting comp segment performance.

Finding #11: There are three types of winning product, items that have high demand and high unit volume, items that have high demand and low unit volume, and items that have low demand and high unit volume. These items do not remain at "winning" status, they decay rapidly (by between 20% and 30% in annual performance), requiring a constant stream of new, winning items to replace existing, winning items.

Finding #12: This business did not find enough new, winning items to replace existing, winning items. This is the primary reason the business is suffering.

Finding #13: New product development is reasonably consistent for high volume merchandise categories.

Finding #14: New product development is in horrific decline for low volume merchandise categories. This is the primary reason the business is struggling - the merchandising team appears to be phasing out new product development in low volume categories, and customers are simply choosing not to purchase as often, as a consequence.

Finding #15: Customer repurchase rates are slightly higher among low price point items. Customer repurchase rates are slightly lower among high price point items. The merchandising team is moving to high price point items, and by doing so, is deflating customer repurchase rates, hurting the future of the business.

Finding #16: High price point items align with loyal customers, and with the Christmas season. As a result, the merchandising team unintentionally interacted with the marketing team in an unfavorable manner. Best customers are encouraged to buy high price point items via discounts and promotions, destroying the beneficial gross margin impact of high priced items.

Finding #17: About 70% of the reason why the business is struggling can be attributed to a phasing out of new item development, especially among low volume merchandise categories. This is the reason the business is failing, no doubt about it. Through a Merchandise Forensics analysis, we have been able to identify the core problem with this business.

Finding #18: This business must ramp up new item development by 80% a year, and hold it at that level for five years, in order to reverse the negative demand trend and return this business to growth. Eighty percent, folks!

A Merchandise Forensics analysis allows us to figure out _why_ a business is struggling. Our current suite of analytical tools are ideally suited for figuring out _why conversion/response rates struggle_. The current set of tools give us a 3 foot view of the business. We need a 30,000 foot view of the business, one provided by a Merchandise Forensics framework.

In this analysis, we clearly see that the Merchandising team made decisions that set the business up for failure. The Merchandising team failed to understand the importance of new items. The Merchandising team cut back on new items in low-volume categories, possibly thinking that cutting back investment in these areas wouldn't impact the big picture.

Unfortunately, this decision set up a series of cascading events that hurt the business. Customers spent less, causing Marketing to ramp up promotions, causing Marketing to spend precious ad dollars on an omnichannel strategy. This propped-up the business for a year, then productivity fell significantly.

In my projects, I find that the situation causing housefile customers to spend less (fewer new products) also harms new customer acquisition, causing a business to acquire fewer new customers, further accelerating demand problems.

A Framework For Success

Maybe it has always been this way, but in the internet era, marketing has been hijacked by campaign analysis. Our software, and our analysts have been designed/trained to evaluate how customers convert. We've been taught to measure the effectiveness of marketing tactics.

This "three foot view" of the world causes us to miss the true reason why businesses succeed or fail. We know why a 30% off plus free shipping email works, we don't know why the business isn't working.

Then, we have the "thought leaders" who provide a "strategic" view of the world at a 300,000 foot level. Sure, we know that mobile will be 72% of the internet in 2020, but who cares? How is that relevant to helping me fix my business next year?

Merchandise is a major reason why businesses succeed or fail. And we know this, intuitively, or we wouldn't get antsy when Apple doesn't innovate as fast as we want them to.

And yet, within our own businesses, we simply ignore merchandise. Why is that? Why don't we care? Oh, I know, it isn't a pleasant experience to sit down with a merchant and get your rear end handed to you because your marketing strategies are allegedly destroying the brand. I've been there. Often. But just because a merchant frightens you in an effort to shift accountability from merchandise to marketing doesn't mean you don't analyze the living daylights out of merchandising performance. This is your responsibility. You are accountable for this. If you don't do it, who will?

It's time to set up a framework.

Each month, run a comp segment analysis. Yes, each month. It's an annual view, no doubt, but you'll get to clearly see when the business is improving, or when the business is struggling. Make sure you publish this report. I don't care if nobody reads it, publish it anyway. Make sure your Executive team gets in the habit of at least receiving it. Offer your strategic thoughts in a brief, summarized manner. If marketing is ramping up promotions, your comp segment analysis will clearly paint the picture - make sure everybody else knows this. If your merchandising team is de-emphasizing a category, and business struggles as a result, make sure every employee in the company knows this.

If you are a CEO, then you have a responsibility to set realistic yet challenging goals for new products. Our analysis showed that the business needed an 80% increase in new products, across the board, and needed a healthy supply of A/B/C items - new A/B/C items are responsible for half of the gain in demand, D/F items are responsible for the other half. So you set goals for your merchandising team, goals that look something like this:

- Exceeds = 120% Increase in A/B/C New Items.
- Meets = 80% Increase in All New Items.
- Missed = < 80% Increase In All New Items.

Next, the CEO needs to set the same new item goals for the marketing team.

Huh? I thought the merchandising team was responsible for new items?

No, marketing is also responsible. Marketing must analyze the performance of new items. When certain new items emerge as potential winners, the marketing team must respond by giving these items featured real estate in email campaigns and landing pages, even the home page for that matter. Repeat - *the marketing team must respond by giving these items featured real estate in email campaigns and landing pages, even the home page for that matter*. If your merchandising team works their tail off identifying potential winning new products, then you (the marketer) cannot freeze them out. Marketing must be an equal partner, giving potential winning new products the exposure they need to achieve A/B/C status.

Next, the CEO needs to hold what I would call a "monthly product evaluation meeting". Marketing, Merchandising, and Creative are invited to these meetings. Egos are not allowed in the room, folks, and blame is not allowed in the room, either. Rather, these are collaborative sessions designed to get Marketing, Merchandising, and Creative actively involved in the evaluation of new, winning merchandise. Your merchandising team has a series of reports they use to evaluate item performance, so bring those reports to the meeting. Your marketing team must bring merchandise forensics reporting to the meeting, nobody else is going to do this. And your creative team should bring conversion data by creative treatment (a perfect use of a web analytics software platform), so that everybody understands how different merchandise presentations enable better conversion/response rates.

As you may know, I am a big fan of what I call "annual analytics", a 30,000 foot view of the business, not the 3 foot view marketing campaigns require, not the 300,000 foot view that thought leaders and strategists operate in. But web analytics is perfect for evaluating new merchandise. Tag new items, and measure the circumstances where new items sell best. Leverage this data to give new items the best possible opportunity to succeed.

We simply have to view new items the same way we view baseball players in the AAA/AA/A framework, or the way we view the draft in the NFL/NBA. In sports, future wins and losses depend upon today's player development philosophy. Given how important future wins and losses are, a ton of energy is consumed on talent evaluation.

In the Merchandise Forensics framework, a similar amount of energy must be spent developing new items. It's just that simple. Our analysis showed that this business is literally being starved of new items, and as a result, customer spend is on the decline. This business, to use the sports analogy, is losing, and must invest in talent in order to succeed in the future.

Does the framework make sense?

Do you understand the importance of cultivating new items? It means everything to the health of a business. Everything.

Do you understand how critical a "comp segment analysis" is? This simple report allowed all the key issues surrounding this business to fall in our lap!

Do you understand the analytics, the reports I presented? These reports are not difficult to create. If your team cannot create them, then please ask me to create them (kevinh@minethatdata.com)! I've analyzed this kind of stuff for twenty or more businesses since January 2012 - this framework identified merchandising problems among eighty percent of the companies I worked with.

The simple example, presented in this booklet, should be more than enough to motivate us to change, to evaluate merchandise productivity. It would be very difficult for users reviewing standard response reporting and web analytics reporting to uncover the issues identified in this booklet. Very, very difficult. Not impossible. Maybe we just need to expand our toolkit just a bit.

I think it is worth the effort. When we can identify an issue that caused 71% of the shortfall observed in a business, we should pay attention to the methodology!

Hire Kevin!

I routinely work with CEOs, CFOs, and CMOs on key marketing/merchandising issues. Since founding MineThatData in 2007, I have worked with more than one hundred retail brands, e-commerce upstarts, and catalog marketers, generating more than fifty million dollars in annual profit opportunity.

My projects typically take four weeks to complete. The data requirements are not onerous, by any means.

To view project costs and data requirements, please visit this link:

http://minethatdata.com/Kevin_Hillstrom_MineThatData_ProjectPricing 2014.pdf

Contact me (kevinh@minethatdata.com) for additional details.

Kevin Hillstrom
President, MineThatData
kevinh@minethatdata.com
Twitter: @minethatdata
Blog: http://blog.minethatdata.com
Website: http://minethatdata.com

Made in the USA
Las Vegas, NV
17 March 2021